A Small Baby Raccoon

Written by Sharon Fear

In the spring, a small baby
raccoon is born.

The mother raccoon looks
like she has a mask.

are sometimes called a cub

The small baby raccoon
has no mask at all.

A baby raccoon is
sometimes called a cub.

In the summer, the small
baby raccoon is still growing.

But now it can climb a tree.

A raccoon can swim very well.

In the fall, the raccoon still hunts for food.

It hunts for small animals.

It also eats eggs, nuts, and seeds.

In the winter, a raccoon curls into a ball and sleeps for a long time.

In the spring, a new small
baby raccoon is born.